FANTASTIC SPORT FACTS

CRICKET

Michael Hurley

Raintree is an imprint of Capstone Global Library Limited, a company incorporated in England and Wales having its registered office at 7 Pilgrim Street, London, EC4V 6LB – Registered company number: 6695582

Edited by Catherine Veitch, Sian Smith,
  and John-Paul Wilkins
Designed by Richard Parker
Picture research by Ruth Blair
Originated by Capstone Global Library Ltd
Printed and bound in China

ISBN 978 1 406 25349 8 (hardback)
16 15 14 13 12
10 9 8 7 6 5 4 3 2 1

British Library Cataloguing in Publication Data
Hurley, Michael.
Cricket. -- (Fantastic sport facts)
796.3'58-dc23
A full catalogue record for this book is available from the British Library.

Acknowledgements
We would like to thank the following for permission to reproduce photographs: Corbis p. 19 (© STR/epa); Getty Images pp. 5 (Gareth Copley), 6 (Popperfoto), 9 (Sanjeev Verma/Hindustan Times), 11 (Hulton Archives/Fox Photos), 12 (Ben Radford), 14 (Hamish Blair/ALLSPORT), 15 (Darren England), 16 (Cameron Spencer), 17 (Clive Rose), 18 (Tom Shaw), 20 (Robert Cianflone), 21 (Matthew Lewis), 22 (ALEXANDER JOE/AFP), 24 (SENA VIDANAGAMA/AFP); Photoshot pp. 7, 26 (© Actionplus), 25 (© Xinhua), 27 (© UPPA); Shutterstock pp. 4 (© Lance Bellers), 10 (© Richard Goldberg), 13 mug (© gillmar), 13 crown (© iadams), 13 cricket ball (© Robyn Mackenzie), 21 (© Sean Gladwell).

Cover photograph of Brian Lara reproduced with permission of Getty Images (OLLY GREENWOOD/AFP), and a cricket ball reproduced with permission of Shutterstock (© Robyn Mackenzie).

Disclaimer

Contents

Some words are printed in bold, **like this**. You can find out what they mean by looking in the glossary.

Cricket basics

There are three types of cricket:

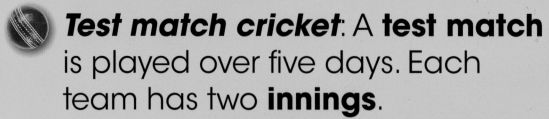 ***Test match cricket***: A **test match** is played over five days. Each team has two **innings**.

One-day cricket: This has a limited number of **overs** (usually 50).

Twenty20 cricket: A shorter version of one-day cricket. Each team has just 20 overs.

Past to present

The first ever cricket **test match** took place in 1877. The game was played between Australia and England. Australia won by 45 **runs**.

Alfred Shaw was England's leading bowler in the match. He took 8 **wickets**, including 5 in the second **innings**.

Sri Lanka played India in the 2011 Cricket World Cup final.

DID YOU KNOW?

The first ever international cricket match was played between the United States and Canada in 1844.

Six sixes

Six **runs** is the most that a batsman can score from each ball. Only four batsmen have ever managed to score six runs from each ball in an **over**.

This table shows the four players who have scored six sixes in an over.

Year	Player	Team	Opponent
1968	G. Sobers	Northamptonshire	Glamorgan
1984	R. Shastri	Bombay	Boroda
2007	H. Gibbs	South Africa	Netherlands
2007	Y. Singh	India	England

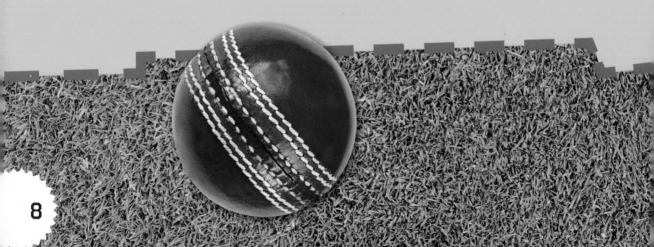

DID YOU KNOW?

When Herschelle Gibbs scored six sixes in 2007, he helped to raise nearly £630,000 for charity.

Longest and shortest

The longest **test match** of all time was played between South Africa and England, in 1938. The match lasted for nine days, and ended in a draw.

FUN FACT

The match had to end when it did, because the England players had to catch a boat home!

The shortest completed test match of all time took place in Melbourne, Australia in 1932. Australia beat South Africa in just 5 hours and 53 minutes!

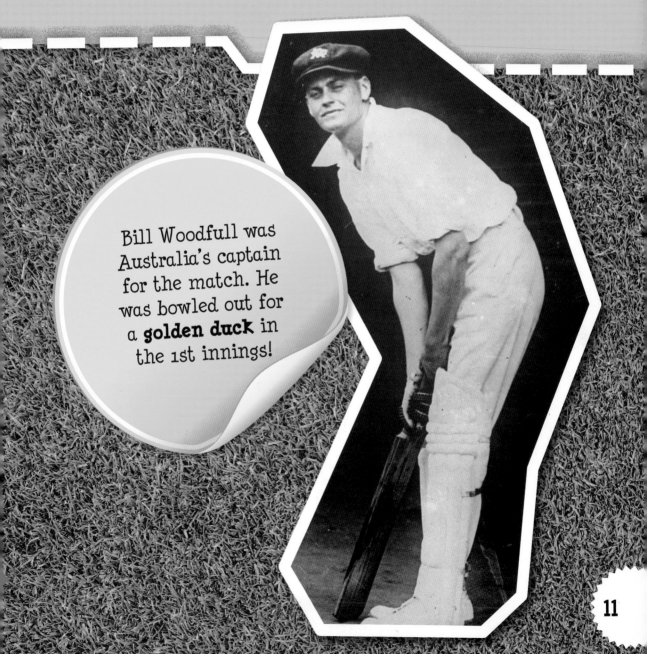

Bill Woodfull was Australia's captain for the match. He was bowled out for a **golden duck** in the 1st innings!

King of Spain

Teammates of England **spin bowler** Ashley Giles had mugs made, which were meant to say "King of spin" on them. Instead of "spin", the mugs had "spain" written on them. It led to Ashley Giles being nicknamed "King of Spain"!

KING OF SPAIN

Brilliant twins

Mark and Steve Waugh were two of Australia's best batsmen. They were also twins. They played in over 100 matches together!

Mark and Steve were also great fielders. Between them, they took 293 catches in test matches.

DID YOU KNOW?

The first female twins to play in the same **test match** were Rosemary and Elizabeth Signal. They played for New Zealand against England in 1984.

The Ashes

The biggest and most famous **rivalry** in cricket is between England and Australia. The first Ashes series took place in 1882. Every two years, the two teams battle it out to win the Ashes.

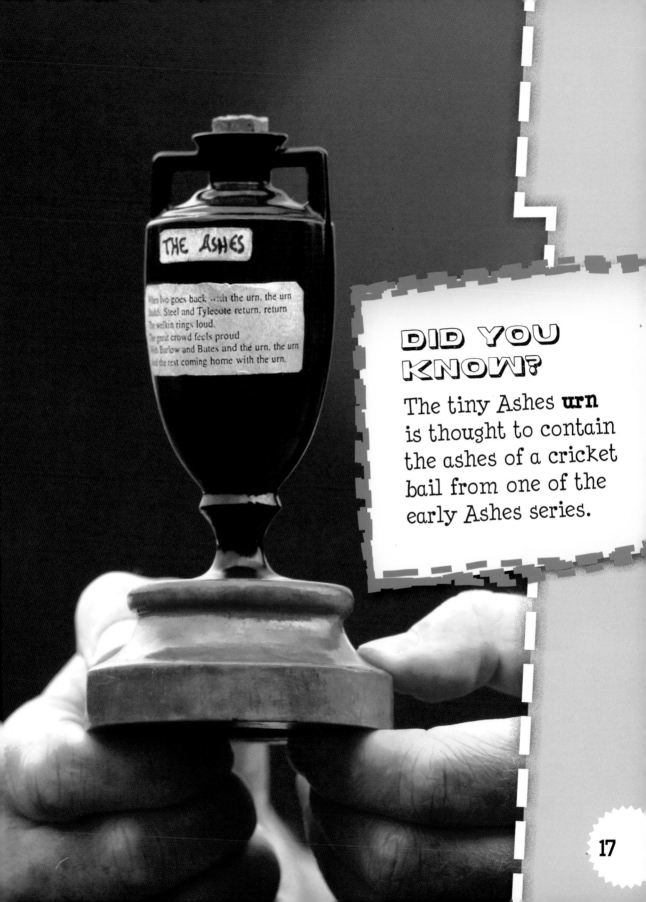

THE ASHES

When Ivo goes back with the urn, the urn
Shall. Steel and Tylecote return, return
The welkin rings loud.
The great crowd feels proud
With Barlow and Bates and the urn, the urn
And the rest coming home with the urn.

DID YOU KNOW?

The tiny Ashes **urn** is thought to contain the ashes of a cricket bail from one of the early Ashes series.

Highest individual score

BATSMEN		BATTING
JACOBS	107	WEST INDIES
LARA	400	TOTAL

REMAINING OVERS

751

60

WKTS

5

RCC

Brian Lara scored the highest individual score in a **test match**. He scored 400 **runs** for the West Indies against England in 2004.

The highest individual score in a **one-day match** was by India's Virender Sehwag. He scored 219 runs.

Sehwag is one of only four batsmen to score over 300 runs twice in test cricket.

DID YOU KNOW?

West Indian cricketer Chris Gayle and Richard Levi of South Africa share the top score in Twenty20 cricket with 117 runs.

Huge crowds

In 1961, 90,800 people packed in to the Melbourne Cricket Ground (MCG) to watch the final day of Australia versus the West Indies. This was the highest attendance ever for a cricket match.

The MCG held the first ever **test match** in 1877.

DID YOU KNOW?

When the rules of cricket were first written in 1744, there were only two stumps. The third stump was introduced in 1775.

Cricket is so popular in India that crowds of up to 100,000 are common.

Highest score

The record for the highest number of **runs** scored in Twenty20 is held by Sri Lanka. They scored 260 when they played Kenya in 2007.

RECORD BREAKERS

Sri Lanka also holds the record for the highest number of runs in a **test match**. They scored 952 when they played India in 1997.

This table shows the top-five team scores:

Team	Opponent	Score	Year
Sri Lanka	India	952	1997
England	Australia	903	1938
England	West Indies	849	1930
West Indies	Pakistan	790	1958
Pakistan	Sri Lanka	765	2009

Great bowlers

India's Anil Kumble collected all ten **wickets** in an **innings** against Pakistan in 1999. Only two players in history have achieved this. England's Jim Laker was the first in 1956.

Great batters

Sachin Tendulkar is one of the greatest batsmen of all time. He has scored an incredible 100 **centuries** in his career.

2

DID YOU KNOW?

England women's cricket captain Charlotte Edwards is one of the world's top cricketers. Edwards has played for her country over 200 times.

Quiz

Are you a superfan or a couch potato? Decide whether the statements below are true or false. Then look at the answers on page 31 and check your score on the fanometer.

1 Sir Garfield Sobers was the first batsman to score six sixes in an **over**.

2 The Ashes began in 1900.

3 The MCG held the first ever cricket **test match** in 1890.

Sri Lankan bowler Muttiah Muralitharan took 700 **wickets** in his career.

5 The first ever Twenty20 international match took place in 2005.

6 Indian batsman Sachin Tendulkar holds the record as the highest **run** scorer in test match history.

FANOMETER

all-rounder

couch potato

1 2 3 4 5 6

superfan

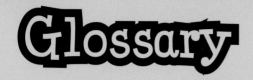

Glossary

century one hundred runs, scored by a batsman in an innings

golden duck when a batsman is bowled out with the first ball they face

innings time when a team or player is batting

one-day match game of cricket of one innings per side, played on a single day

over series of six balls bowled by a bowler, all from the same end of the pitch

rivalry when two people or teams compete against each other

run point scored by a batsman

spin bowler bowler who spins the ball

technique special way of doing something

test match international cricket match of two innings per side, played over five days

urn type of vase for holding ashes. The Ashes are kept in an urn.

wicket when a bowler gets a batsman out

Find out more

Books

World Cricket Records 2012, Chris Hawkes (Carlton Books Ltd, 2011)

Cricket (Great Sporting Events), Clive Gifford (Franklin Watts, 2011)

Website

www.espncricinfo.com/games/content/site/
Play a selection of online cricket games on this website.

Quiz answers

1) True (see page 8).
2) False. The first Ashes series was played in 1882 (see page 16).
3) False. The MCG held the first cricket test match in 1877 (see page 20).
4) False. Muralitharan took 800 wickets in his career (see page 25).
5) True. Australia faced New Zealand in the first Twenty20 match in 2005.
6) True. Tendulkar broke Brian Lara's record in 2008.

Index